The
Iroquois Indians

by Bill Lund

Reading Consultant:
Alice Bomberry
Education Coordinator, Woodland Cultural Centre
Judy Harris
Assistant Curator, Woodland Cultural Centre

Bridgestone Books
an Imprint of Capstone Press

Bridgestone Books are published by Capstone Press
818 North Willow Street, Mankato, Minnesota 56001
Copyright © 1997 by Capstone Press
Printed in the United States of America

Library of Congress Cataloging-in-Publication Data
Lund, Bill, 1954-.
    The Iroquois Indians/by Bill Lund.
    p. cm.--(Native peoples)
    Includes bibliographical references and index.
    Summary: Discusses the Iroquois as a modern group with a unique history and its own
    special practices and customs.
    ISBN 1-56065-480-5
    1. Iroquois Indians--History--Juvenile literature. 2. Iroquois Indians--Social life and
    customs--Juvenile literature.
    [1. Iroquois Indians. 2. Indians of North America.] I. Title.
    II. Series: Lund, Bill, 1954-   Native peoples.

E99.I7L86 1997
973'.049755--dc21
                                                96-51504
                                                  CIP
                                                  AC

Photo credits
Unicorn/Richard Baker, cover, 6, 14
Woodland Cultural Centre, 8, 10, 18
MN/DOT, 12
FPG, 16
John Fadden, courtesy of the Iroquois Indian Museum, Haves Cave, NY, 20

Table of Contents

Map

Canada

U.S.A.

Mexico

Where the Iroquois used to live

Fast Facts

Today many Iroquois Indians live like most other North Americans. In the past, they practiced a different way of life. Their food, homes, and clothes helped make them special. These facts tell how the Iroquois once lived.

Food: The Iroquois ate corn, beans, squash, and other vegetables and fruit. They also ate fish, birds, and animals.

Home: They lived in a longhouse. A longhouse is a long building with a rounded roof.

Clothing: Iroquois men wore deerskin leggings, shirts, and moccasins. The women wore leggings, shirts, skirts, and moccasins.

Language: There are six major Iroquois groups. Their languages are part of the Iroquoian language family.

Special Events: The Green Corn Harvest and the Midwinter Renewal are favorite events. The Iroquois have many special events throughout the year.

Past Location: The Iroquois used to live in the northeastern United States and southeastern Canada.

Current Location: They now live on reservations in the northeastern United States and on reserves in southeastern Canada.

People of Peace

The Iroquois are a group of North American Indians. Many nations make up the Iroquois. A nation is a group of people. These people have the same language, customs, and government. A custom is a way of doing things. The Mohawk, Oneida, Onondaga, Cayuga, Seneca, and Tuscarora are Iroquois nations.

The Iroquois have always lived in the northeastern United States and southeastern Canada. Today many live on Canadian reserves or United States reservations. A reserve or reservation is land set aside for Native Americans. Other Iroquois live in towns and cities throughout the world.

Today Iroquois people live like their non-Indian neighbors. Yet they still enjoy many of their old traditions. A tradition is a practice continued over many years.

Dancing is a tradition the Iroquois still enjoy.

Homes, Food, and Clothing

Long ago, the Iroquois lived in buildings called longhouses. A longhouse was long with a rounded roof. Men built a longhouse by bending trees. The trees made a frame. Then the men covered the frame with tree bark.

Women made clothing, household tools, and food. They also farmed, cooked the food, and stored food for winter.

The women raised crops such as corn, beans, and squash. These crops are called the Three Sisters. The Three Sisters were often cooked into a dish called succotash. People in North America still eat it today.

The men also helped gather food for the village. They hunted and fished.

Iroquois clothing varied with the season. Their clothes were made from animal skins. Both men and women wore leggings, moccasins, and shirts. The women sometimes wore skirts.

Iroquois women raised corn, beans, and squash.

The Iroquois Family

A longhouse was shared by members of a clan. A clan is a large family group. Clans were named after animals. Some clans were named after bears and beavers.

After marriage, a couple would live with the wife's clan. Children became members of their mother's clan.

Iroquois women have always been highly respected. The oldest woman of the clan is the clan mother. In most Iroquois nations, a clan mother chooses her clan's leaders. Only men are chosen. Leaders from each clan come together in meetings. They make decisions for their nation.

The leaders talk with their clan mothers and clan before each meeting. The clan mothers give them advice on important issues. A leader must respect the rules and his clan mother's advice. If not, she can remove him from office.

A longhouse was shared by members of a clan.

Religious Life

The Iroquois believe in a Creator of all things. The Iroquois thank the Creator for all things in nature. Their religion is called Longhouse religion.

The Iroquois also believe in spirits. Spirits are present in all living things. Some spirits are evil. These spirits bring sickness and bad luck.

The Iroquois use masks to scare away these evil spirits. The masks are carved from living basswood trees. Members of the Medicine Mask Society wear the masks. The Medicine Mask Society is a group that performs healing ceremonies. A ceremony is an official practice.

Europeans taught Christianity to many Iroquois people. Christianity is a religion based on the teachings of Christ. Today some Iroquois are members of Christian faiths. Other Iroquois still practice the Longhouse religion. The Iroquois still respect all things in nature.

Masks are carved from living basswood trees.

The League of Nations

Long ago, the Iroquois nations often fought with one another. The Creator gave two men a dream of peace. The men were the Peacemaker and Hiawatha. They told the Iroquois nations of their dream for unity. Unity means that groups of people come together in peace.

In the late 1400s, five Iroquois nations came together. They formed the League of Nations. The Mohawk, Oneida, Onondaga, Cayuga, and Seneca joined the league. In 1722, the Tuscarora nation joined the league.

The League of Nations helped the Iroquois keep peace. Each nation's clan mother chose one person to speak for them. They made important decisions about wars, treaties, and land rights. A treaty is an official agreement between two nations.

This man is a member of the Cayuga nation.

Iroquois and the Settlers

In the 1500s, Europeans began arriving. The Iroquois traded animal furs for European cloth, metal, and guns. They traded with the Dutch, English, and French.

The Revolutionary War (1776-1783) began between England and the American colonies. A colony is a group of people who settle in a distant land. They remain under the control of their native country.

The Iroquois did not want to be in the war. Later, they joined. But the Iroquois could not decide which group to help. So each nation decided for itself. Some groups sided with the American colonies. Other groups helped the English. War weakened the Iroquois League of Nations. Today it is strong again.

In the 1700s, European settlers copied the idea of the league. The United States Congress is like the League of Nations. The United Nations is also like the Iroquois league.

The Iroquois traded animal furs with the Europeans.

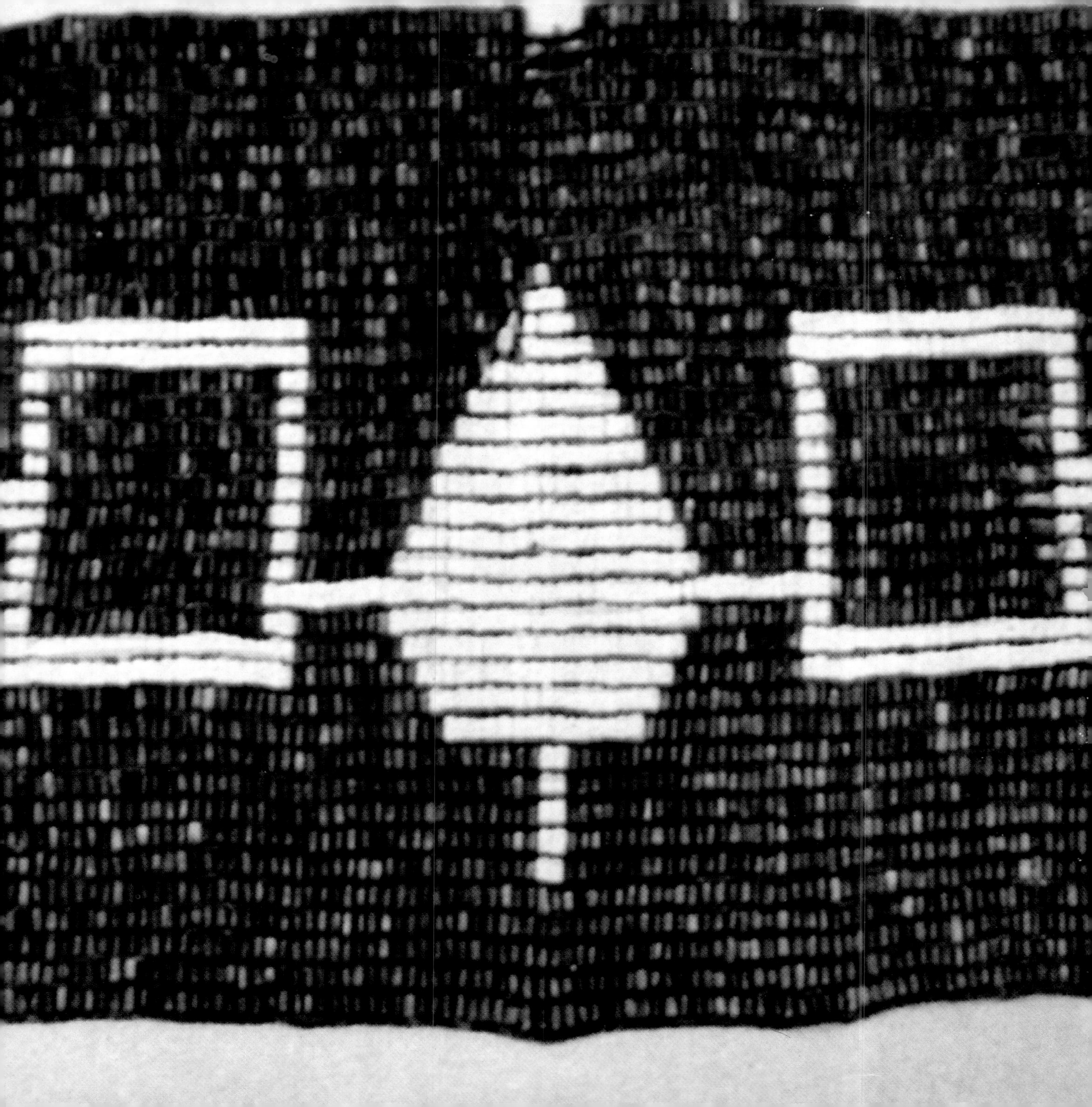

Wampum

In the past, many Iroquois used wampum. Wampum is made from shells. The shells are cut into beads. Then a small hole is drilled into each bead. These beads are then placed on strings. Many strings are sewn together to make a complete wampum belt.

The Iroquois used wampum for different reasons. They gave wampum belts when they made a promise to someone.

Wampum belts were also used to show a person's position or title. The great Circle wampum showed a Chief's position. Treaties and other important events were recorded on wampum.

Today some Iroquois still use wampum. It is used in ceremonies and for belts. The Iroquois also still give it when they make a promise.

Wampum was used to record important events.

How the Earth Was Made

Iroquois told many stories called legends. Legends were told to explain something. One Iroquois legend tells how people were made.

Long ago, the world was covered by water. Far above the world lived the Happy Spirits. In the land of Happy Spirits was a giant tree.

One day, the Happy Spirits' Chief pulled up the tree. This left a hole where the tree once stood. He saw the world of water below. The Chief sent his daughter into that world. He carefully dropped her into the hole.

The water animals saw her floating down. They called her Sky Woman. They created the earth on a turtle's back. Birds helped her land.

After a time, Sky Woman gave birth to twins. She died soon after. Good Twin hung his mother's head in the sky. It became the sun. He also made good things. Evil Twin made bad things. They fought to control the world.

Good Twin and Evil Twin fought to control the world.

Hands On: Make Wampum

Wampum is a string of beads made from shells. The Iroquois used wampum for promises, to show position or title, and to record important events. You can make wampum using macaroni noodles.

What You Need

Uncooked macaroni
Blue and red food coloring
Rubbing alcohol
Yarn or string, about 18 inches (46 centimeters) long
Small bowl
Spoon
Newspaper

What You Do

1. Pour about 1 cup of rubbing alcohol into the bowl.
2. Add blue and red food coloring until the rubbing alcohol turns dark purple.
3. Soak half of the macaroni in the purple rubbing alcohol. Wait until the macaroni turns purple. Leave the macaroni in only long enough to color it.
4. Spoon out the colored macaroni. Let it dry on newspaper.
5. String the colored and uncolored macaroni on the yarn or string. Make a pattern.
6. Tie the ends of the string together. You can wear your wampum as a necklace.

Words to Know

longhouse (LAWNG-houss)—a long, narrow house usually for members of one clan

reservation (rez-ur-VAY-shuhn)—land set aside for Native Americans in the United States

reserve (ri-ZURV)—land set aside for Native Americans in Canada

succotash (SUH-cah-tahsh)—a traditional food made of corn, beans, and squash

wampum (WAM-puhm)—strings of shell beads used for promises, to show position or title, and to record important events

Read More

Graymont, Barbara. *The Iroquois*. Indians of North America. New York: Chelsea House, 1988.

Sneve, Virginia Driving Hawk. *The Iroquois*. New York: Holiday House, 1995.

Wolfson, Evelyn. *The Iroquois: People of the Northeast*. Brookfield, Conn.: The Millbrook Press, 1992.

Useful Addresses

Seneca Iroquois National Museum
Broad Street Extension
Salamanca, NY 14779

Woodland Cultural Centre
184 Mohawk Street
P.O. Box 1506
Brantford, ON N3T 5V6
Canada

Internet Sites

Sainte Marie among the Iroquois
http://maple.lemoyne.edu:80/~milleram/
saintemarie.html

Native American Indian
http://indy4.fdl.cc.mn.us/~isk/

Index